Bill Huebsch

PRAYING THE STATIONS WITH SAINT JOHN XXIII

TWENTY-THIRD PUBLICATIONS *A Division of Bayard*
One Montauk Avenue, Suite 200 • New London, CT 06320 • (800) 321-0411 • www.23rdpublications.com
ISBN 978-1-62785-004-9 • Copyright ©2013 Bill Huebsch. All rights reserved. No part of this publication may be reproduced
in any manner without prior written permission of the publisher. Write to the Permissions Editor. Printed in the U.S.A.

INTRODUCTION

His name at baptism was Angelo Roncalli. He grew up in a large Catholic farm family in northern Italy. There was hard, manual labor mixed with family celebrations blended with life in the local parish. For young Angelo, these elements of life formed a seamless garment. The way to holiness was not any one of these without the others.

In this family setting he learned to die to himself and to give himself to others. Here he learned how God touched his life every day. He learned how to be "the big one" with his brothers and sisters, parents, aunts, and uncles. He learned how to sometimes accept with humility the lower place at the family table.

He knew the Paschal Mystery—the living, dying, and rising of Christ—in his very bones. The pathway to holiness, this saintly man knew, was the same kind of self-giving love. Later, when he accepted assignments as an ambassador of the pope to faraway places, and when he came back to Rome to be elected pope himself, these lessons served him well. He embraced others freely. He opened wide his arms to all. And he developed a strong sense of compassion for everyone. He blended those three lessons of childhood: how to work hard, how to celebrate freely, and how to rely on his faith. He was so authentic that he drew others to him like a magnet.

When this humble pilgrim called the universal Church to renew itself at the Second Vatican Council, the whole world responded! From every corner of the earth came Catholics, but also other Christians, Jews, and even non-believers. The Council itself declared what he believed: that we are immersed in the dying and rising of Christ, and this is the pathway we must follow (Constitution on the Liturgy #6 and on the Church #42).

You are about to pray the Way of the Cross with this man, Pope Saint John XXIII, as your companion. Please bear in mind that, as Pope John knew so well, these stations are not merely a series of historical events that are now done and over. This is a living story, one that laces itself into your own life. This is what the call to holiness means: the Way of the Cross is a story about Christ, yes, but also one about us.

Parishes and individual Christians often pray these stations once a week during Lent, but it makes sense to pray them throughout all the seasons of the year. It is appropriate to begin your prayer with the Sign of the Cross. You may also wish to end each station by praying the Our Father or Hail Mary.

Scripture texts in this work are taken from *The Message: The Bible in Contemporary Language (Catholic/Ecumenical edition)*, © 2013 (Chicago, IL: ACTA Publications). Used with permission.

The First Station

Announcement of the Station

LEADER   The First Station: Jesus is condemned to death

Dialogue

LEADER   We adore you, O Christ, and we bless you.

ALL   Because by your holy cross, you have redeemed the world.

LEADER   Jesus, Lord and Giver of Life, we know that you prayed in the Garden of Olives for the power to undertake the difficult work to which God called you. We know that you loved life and feared death, just as we do. And we know that your disciples have always found it difficult to watch and pray at your side, sometimes lacking the faith to follow your call. When you were condemned, the strength you gained in that garden remained with you. May such strength also be given to us when we are judged or condemned for choosing love over hate and light over darkness.

Response (PSALM 102:1–4, 8)

ALL   GOD, listen! Listen to my prayer,
    listen to the pain in my cries.
Don't turn your back on me
    just when I need you so desperately.
Pay attention! This is a cry for *help*!
    And hurry—this can't wait!
I'm wasting away to nothing,
    I'm burning up with fever.

I'm a ghost of my former self,
    half-consumed already by terminal illness.
All day long my enemies taunt me,
    while others just curse.

Reflection

LEADER In calling the Second Vatican Council, Pope John XXIII called the world's Catholics to struggle with many important issues in the Church. Pope John often prayed to be faithful to what God wants for us. He risked the judgment and condemnation of those who did not want a council. He stood up for what he knew was God's will for us as the Church. In the end, Vatican II reformed the Church to more faithfully reflect the mission of Jesus in today's world. For us who are members of this Church today, it is now our task to work diligently to continue this renewal and extend the power of Christ to all the world.

A momentary, sacred pause…

LEADER Jesus, give us the special grace and power we need to remain faithful to you and your mission in the world. May we bear judgments against us with the same courage you did. Make our lives a witness to your word and set our hearts on fire with great love. Amen.

The Second Station

Announcement of the Station

LEADER   The Second Station: Jesus carries his cross

Dialogue

LEADER   We adore you, O Christ, and we bless you.

ALL   Because by your holy cross, you have redeemed the world.

LEADER   Jesus, it's difficult for us to imagine how painful it must have been for you to be betrayed to death by one of your closest friends. And even more painful must have been the form of betrayal: a kiss! And yet you remained loving through it all. You accepted the cross and never stopped loving even those who betrayed, mocked, and killed you. May your fidelity to love in the midst of hate empower us to do likewise and to never lose sight of our own divine call. As you set forth on the pathway to Calvary with the cross on your shoulders, so we also now set forth on the pathway to holiness, carrying the cross we also have been given in our lives.

Response (PSALM 37:1–6)

ALL   Don't bother your head with braggarts
or wish you could succeed like the wicked.
In no time they'll shrivel like grass clippings
and wilt like cut flowers in the sun.
Get insurance with GOD and do a good deed,
settle down and stick to your last.

Keep company with GOD,
   get in on the best.
Open up before GOD, keep nothing back;
   he'll do whatever needs to be done:
He'll validate your life in the clear light of day
   and stamp you with approval at high noon.

Reflection

LEADER One of the greatest dangers of modern life is that we grow
so accustomed to comfort and security that, without mean-
ing to, we betray the spirit of the gospels. Pope John XXIII
was keenly aware of this. Because of his witness, Vatican
II reemphasized for members of the Church that baptism
commits us to ministry. It commits us to reach out to others, to love in the midst of hate, to remain faithful as Jesus
did—even to carrying our daily cross. And in the end, it
commits us to risk rejection and security in order to work
for justice and live in peace. For in the end, what matters
most is not financial gain or personal prestige, but that we
remain faithful to Christ.

A momentary, sacred pause…

LEADER Jesus, we face the daily dying of our own cross with great
hope and not with fear. Because of your sacrifice, we are
empowered to live with self-giving love. Create in us hearts
ready to empty ourselves and follow in your footsteps.
Amen.

The Third Station

Announcement of the Station

LEADER   The Third Station: Jesus falls the first time

Dialogue

LEADER   We adore you, O Christ, and we bless you.

ALL   Because by your holy cross, you have redeemed the world.

LEADER   Jesus, you stood before the Sanhedrin, a council of your own people, and faced their terrible judgment. They saw you, but rejected your word of love and your lifestyle of repentance and faith. They did not believe in your healing and teaching power. And they did not see in your face the very face of God. As you walked those first steps on the road to Calvary, this first fall did not change your loving heart or reduce your commitment to your mission. May we ourselves, here and now, show the same resolve when we stumble. May we see the face of God in the faces of all around us, even those we find it most difficult to love.

Response (PSALM 36:1–4)

ALL   The God-rebel tunes in to sedition—
    all ears, eager to sin.
He has no regard for God,
    he stands insolent before him.
He has smooth-talked himself into believing
That his evil will never be noticed.
Words gutter from his mouth, dishwater dirty.

Can't remember when he did anything decent.
Every time he goes to bed,
 he fathers another evil plot.
When he's loose on the streets, nobody's safe.
He plays with fire
 and doesn't care who gets burned.

Reflection

LEADER   It was one of Pope John's dreams that Vatican II would open
the windows and the doors of the Church again. For many
centuries, the Church's doors had been closed and the leaders of the Church had been in the business of judging others,
of deciding who was worthy to receive God's love and who
was not. Like Jesus had been, many people were judged
harshly during those years. Pope John trusted that, with the
help of Christ and the Holy Spirit, the Church would not
stumble and fall but be made stronger—as Christ was on his
way to Calvary. Today the Church sees itself as a loving sign
of the reign of God on earth. God, we know, loves all without
distinction. As such, the Church now embraces all who come
to join in the banquet.

A momentary, sacred pause…

LEADER   Help us when we stumble and fall, Jesus, Lord of life and
love. When the inevitable happens and we commit that old
sin again, or when we see a chance to love and reject it, or
when we treat others harshly on purpose, stand beside us
with your loving forgiveness, and help us get up and get
back on the road to you. Amen.

The Fourth Station

Announcement of the Station

LEADER   The Fourth Station: Jesus meets his mother

Dialogue

LEADER   We adore you, O Christ, and we bless you.

ALL   Because by your holy cross, you have redeemed the world.

LEADER   Jesus, we know that you suffered much rejection and much hatred for being the person God had called you to be. We know that when people around you saw love, they rejected it—and you with it! Your own mother must have felt great pain in her heart. But what could have been more painful for you than to see her suffer? And yet, she too trusted in your never-ending love. May we risk this same level of rejection as we stand up for justice, for what is right, for those who are living as God calls them to live. May we allow Mary, your beloved mother, to walk beside us on our pathway to holiness.

Response (PSALM 38:1–4)

ALL   Take a deep breath, GOD; calm down—
        don't be so hasty with your punishing rod.
    Your sharp-pointed arrows of rebuke draw blood;
        my backside smarts from your caning.
    I've lost twenty pounds in two months
        because of your accusation.

My bones are brittle as dry sticks because of my sin.
I'm swamped by my bad behavior,
    collapsed under gunnysacks of guilt.

Reflection

LEADER Pope John loved his family throughout his life, especially
his dear mother. She was a poor farm woman, a person who
worked hard day in and day out, living without the comfort available to most of society. But her example of faith
in the midst of difficulty, of generosity even when there
wasn't enough to go around, of kindness to strangers, and
of an open heart to all who came to her door, became Pope
John's own way of life. At Vatican II, all were welcomed:
Catholic, Protestant, Anglican, Orthodox, Jewish, Mus-
lim—all sisters and brothers, all related to the People of
God. May Mary's example lead us to the same kind of love
for all the people of the world.

A momentary, sacred pause…

LEADER Mary, we stand beside you now as we offer ourselves to
Christ. May your fidelity as the first disciple be the example
we follow in our own lives. May we bear our sorrows with
dignity and see embedded in them the call to holiness.
Amen.

The Fifth Station

Announcement of the Station

LEADER   The Fifth Station: Simon of Cyrene helps Jesus
to carry the cross

Dialogue

LEADER   We adore you, O Christ, and we bless you.

ALL   Because by your holy cross, you have redeemed the world.

LEADER   There were many people on your way of the cross, Jesus.
And here is one who stooped to help you. He went the extra mile to relieve you of your burden. Throughout it all you
remained faithful to your mission. You stood in the midst
of a society of fear, anger, and aggression—but you stood
there as a person of peace, love, and faith. May we also
stand upright at the time of our own judgment in society.
May we have your courage and the strength of your soul
when we ourselves are faced with anger, fear, and aggression. And may we help others as Simon helped you.

Response (PSALM 35:15–18)

ALL   But when I was down they threw a party!
All the nameless riffraff of the town came
  chanting insults about me.
Like barbarians desecrating a shrine,
  they destroyed my reputation.
GOD, how long are you going
  to stand there doing nothing?

Save me from their brutalities;
  everything I've got is being thrown to the lions.
I will give you full credit when everyone gathers for worship;
When the people turn out in force I will say my Hallelujahs.

Reflection

LEADER   When we follow Jesus carefully and faithfully, we live in such a way that the society around us will be threatened. Those who have chosen to live with fear, anger, and aggression will see love in us and reject it. They will not be able to see through it to find Christ. This was Pope John XXIII's dream: that we would replace hatred and division with love, despite the cost. When Vatican II called us to activity in the world, it was calling us to this radical form of love, to going the extra mile as Simon did for Jesus. Many times, therefore, when we work for justice, love, peace, and goodness, we will ironically encounter the terrible judgments of people, people who know better but don't have the courage to support us publicly.

A momentary, sacred pause…

Communal Prayer

ALL   Jesus, you accepted the help of Simon of Cyrene, a stranger who was called on to help you carry your cross. May we likewise accept help from the pastors of the Church as well as our own friends and family when we need it in order to carry the cross given to us. Amen.

The Sixth Station

Announcement of the Station

LEADER   The Sixth Station: Veronica wipes the face of Jesus

Dialogue

LEADER   We adore you, O Christ, and we bless you.

ALL   Because by your holy cross, you have redeemed the world.

LEADER   Jesus, we have already walked with you through judgment and condemnation. Now we stand as witnesses to your suffering as Veronica steps forward to comfort you, all in the name of love. She sees you, not as a criminal or a danger, but as a fellow human being in need of help. She must have asked, "How can this go on? How can people hurt each other so violently?" We ourselves ask that question when we see senseless violence and meanness. May we who have the power to hurt others—which is all of us—refuse to do so. May we become women and men of love instead.

Response (PSALM 27:1–3, 13–14)

ALL   Light, space, zest—that's GOD!
So, with him on my side I'm fearless,
   afraid of no one and nothing.
When vandal hordes ride down ready to eat me alive,
Those bullies and toughs fall flat on their faces.
When besieged, I'm calm as a baby.
When all hell breaks loose, I'm collected and cool.
I'm sure now I'll see God's goodness in the exuberant earth.

Stay with GOD!
    Take heart. Don't quit.
    I'll say it again: Stay with GOD.

Reflection

LEADER   How easy it is for us to turn to one another with love.
And yet, how difficult sometimes it is for us to love those
who are closest to us—in our own homes, and among
our colleagues and closest friends. How easy for us to
mock each other, to "beat" one another with complaints,
meanness, and criticisms. In his journal, Pope John spoke
about how difficult it is to accept the unkindness of others
while remaining charitable ourselves. But he also knew
how essential it is for us on the Christian journey to do so.
Vatican II urged us to live in peace and love with each other.
Recognizing that the reign of God can be established only
when such peace prevails, it sounded the loud call to us all
to live lives of holiness, which means lives where we avoid
treating each other as Christ was treated by the soldiers. It
means we should go out of our way to affirm and support
each other instead.

A momentary, sacred pause…

LEADER   Open us to one another, Oh Christ, Lord of love. Open our
hearts so that love can flow freely from them. Give us the
grace to overcome what stops us from loving each other,
and let us follow the example of Veronica. Amen.

The Seventh Station

Announcement of the Station

LEADER   The Seventh Station: Jesus falls the second time

Dialogue

LEADER   We adore you, O Christ, and we bless you.

ALL   Because by your holy cross, you have redeemed the world.

LEADER   At this point in the way of the cross, we encounter Jesus
undertaking a terrible journey, a path through darkness.
How could you trust in God when the events of your life
are crashing down around you? How could anyone believe
that God is gracious when death awaits us at the end of the
road? It was just at this point in Jesus' journey of faith, how-
ever, where he showed the most courage and strength. He
knew God had not abandoned him. He knew he still lived
in love. And he knew this journey would bring him to life
everlasting. May we likewise be willing to bear—with and
for one another—all the needs of the modern world. May
we be moved to work with the poor, to visit the impris-
oned, to fight for justice at every occasion possible, and to
lead the march for peace.

Response (PSALM 77:1–4, 8–10)

ALL   I yell out to my God, I yell with all my might,
I yell at the top of my lungs. He listens.
I found myself in trouble and went looking for my Lord;
my life was an open wound that wouldn't heal.

When friends said, "Everything will turn out all right,"
I didn't believe a word they said.
I remember God—and shake my head.
I bow my head—then wring my hands.
I'm awake all night—not a wink of sleep;
Has God forgotten his manners?
Has he angrily stalked off and left us?
"Just my luck," I said. "The High God goes out of business
just the moment I need him."

Reflection

LEADER   Pope John XXIII knew he was dying more than a year
before his death. Like Jesus, he loved life and did not want
to die. Vatican II had just opened, and he had hoped to see
its work completed. But, also like Jesus, Pope John allowed
his impending death to shape his life. Learning about
cancer can seem like a pretty hard fall, as Jesus experienced
on his way of the cross. But it was only after he was told
how serious his cancer was that Pope John undertook the
writing of some of his most important work. And, in the
end, Vatican II remained faithful to Pope John's spirit even
after his death.

A momentary, sacred pause…

LEADER   Jesus, you know our hearts and minds. You know how
difficult it is for us to bear some of life's burdens—illness,
death, loss, and sadness. Walk with us on our journey, O
Lord, and give us the grace to be as faithful as you were.
Amen.

The Eighth Station

Announcement of the Station

LEADER   The Eighth Station: Jesus meets the women of Jerusalem

Dialogue

LEADER   We adore you, O Christ, and we bless you.

ALL   Because by your holy cross, you have redeemed the world.

LEADER   Jesus, we remember how generous you were to those around you during your life, how you touched and healed all who came asking for help. We remember as well the power of your presence and the astonishment of the crowds when they heard your teaching. You led the people to freedom and guided them to know their own souls. So here in this moment on your way of the cross, you received the help of these wonderful women, strangers to you. May we likewise receive help when we most need it—and give help to those around us.

Response (PSALM 86:1–7)

ALL   Bend an ear, GOD; answer me.
   I am one miserable wretch!
Keep me safe—haven't I lived a good life?
   Help your servant—I'm depending on you!
You're my God; have mercy on me.
   I count on you from morning to night.
Give your servant a happy life;
   I put myself in your hands!

18

You're well-known as good and forgiving,
   bighearted to all who ask for help.
Pay attention, GOD, to my prayer;
   bend down and listen to my cry for help.
Every time I'm in trouble I call on you,
   confident that you'll answer.

Reflection

LEADER It was the central concern of the Church for many centuries that each member should care for and save his or her own soul. But at Vatican II the focus of how we reach salvation shifted for us. Now we are concerned to help establish the reign of God on earth and save each other's souls as well. We seek to animate the world with the Spirit of Christ. It was Pope John's desire that all Christians—Catholic, Protestant, Orthodox, or Anglican—come together to do this work. He sought an end to the barriers that once divided us. So it's no longer our own souls that we seek to save. Just as these women helped Jesus on his way, so we too are called to help one another on the pathway to holiness.

A momentary, sacred pause…

LEADER Jesus, help us to see the needs of those around us who are suffering in silence or invisibility. Open our eyes and ears to see and hear the cries of the poor and vulnerable. Give our hands the strength needed to offer comfort to them. Amen.

The Ninth Station

LEADER   The Ninth Station: Jesus falls the third time

Dialogue

LEADER   We adore you, O Christ, and we bless you.

ALL   Because by your holy cross, you have redeemed the world.

LEADER   Time after time, Jesus stumbled and fell on his way to
Calvary. The work of dying to self is equally difficult for
us. Embedded in the events and people of our own lives is
a summons to love, to give of ourselves. We know that we
stumble on the pathway to holiness, but because of Jesus'
strength and grace, we get up and go on. May we take courage from this moment on the way of the cross and refuse to
abandon our call to love.

Response (PSALM 91:1–7)

ALL   You who sit down in the High God's presence,
  spend the night in Shaddai's shadow,
Say this: "GOD, you're my refuge.
  I trust in you and I'm safe!"
That's right—he rescues you from hidden traps,
  shields you from deadly hazards.
His huge outstretched arms protect you—
  under them you're perfectly safe;
  his arms fend off all harm.
Fear nothing—not wild wolves in the night,

not flying arrows in the day,
Not disease that prowls through the darkness,
not disaster that erupts at high noon.
Even though others succumb all around,
drop like flies right and left,
no harm will even graze you.

Reflection

LEADER In bringing together all the people of the Church for Vatican II, Pope John hoped to unleash the Spirit on the world of today to help all people come to know Jesus and the salvation he offers us. The fall on Jesus' way to Calvary, Pope John knew, might have been a fall any one of us could experience. If we live in selfishness and violence, then even greater evils will come upon us. If we do not become peace-makers, then we can expect war. And if we do not embrace God's will for us today, then we will live outside the reign of God. But good Pope John trusted in the Spirit to bear us up. He believed that if we acted together as the People of God, we could not fall.

A momentary, sacred pause…

LEADER Oh God of power and might, you have the power to bear us up, to strengthen us for the journey of faith. Come to us now and lead us to freedom and love. Amen.

The Tenth Station

LEADER   The Tenth Station: Jesus is stripped of his clothing

Dialogue

LEADER   We adore you, O Christ, and we bless you.

ALL   Because by your holy cross, you have redeemed the world.

LEADER   Jesus, the clarity of your vision allowed you to recognize goodness even in the midst of hate and evil. And your ever-present charity allowed you to offer love in the midst of violence and death. Even when they disgraced you with this terrible indignity, your heart did not move to hate. In just a few moments, you would offer forgiveness and kindness to the criminal crucified with you, extending the reign of God to all who seem initially to be living outside your reign. May we also be attentive to goodness in this way even when meanness and indignity seem to be all around us, and may we also offer love in the face of hate.

Response (PSALM 25:1–5)

ALL   My head is high, GOD, held high;
I'm looking to you, GOD;
No hangdog skulking for me.
I've thrown in my lot with you;
You won't embarrass me, will you?
Or let my enemies get the best of me?
Don't embarrass any of us

Who went out on a limb for you.
It's the traitors who should be humiliated.
Show me how you work, GOD;
School me in your ways.
Take me by the hand;
Lead me down the path of truth.
You are my Savior, aren't you?

Reflection

LEADER   There was a time in the Catholic Church when all those who did not believe as we did were considered incapable of ever reaching Heaven. These outsiders were considered sinners and heretics—and sometimes they were hounded out of our communities or even killed in the name of Christ. Many of these people were Jews, but they might also have been Muslims, Buddhists, Native peoples, or others. Even Protestants were treated with indignity instead of love. But in calling Vatican II, Pope John explicitly included all of these others in his embrace. He considered them precious and loved children of God.

A momentary, sacred pause…

LEADER   Jesus, forgive us our trespasses—for the times when we have stripped others of their good name, dignity, or rights. Forgive us for treating your brothers and sisters in the way that you were treated on your way of the cross. Amen.

The Eleventh Station

Announcement of the Station

LEADER   The Eleventh Station: Jesus is crucified

Dialogue

LEADER   We adore you, O Christ, and we bless you.

ALL   Because by your holy cross, you have redeemed the world.

LEADER   Jesus, your insight and understanding of what God wants for us and for the world was so firm, so clear, and so deep within you that you could do nothing other than allow yourself to be crucified for it. Your mission was in such direct opposition to the forces of your culture and religious leaders. Your vision drove you to radical belief. May we possess even a fraction of that dedication. May we believe with the same conviction that empowered you. May we accept our own dying, both at the end of life and in our daily call to love.

Response (PSALM 22:1–8)

ALL   God, God … my God!
Why did you dump me miles from nowhere?
Doubled up with pain, I call to God all the day long.
No answer. Nothing.
I keep at it all night, tossing and turning.
And you! Are you indifferent, above it all,
leaning back on the cushions of Israel's praise?
We know you were there for our parents:
they cried for your help and you gave it;

they trusted and lived a good life.
And here I am, a nothing—an earthworm,
    something to step on, to squash.
Everyone pokes fun at me;
    they make faces at me, they shake their heads:
"Let's see how GOD handles this one;
    since God likes him so much, let *him* help him!"

Reflection

LEADER The vocation of the Christian man or woman has a new focus since Pope John called the world to a clearer vision of justice at Vatican II. We humans have often nailed each other to the cross of poverty, disease, and illiteracy. Where once it was enough for us to give a few nickels in charity for the poor, Vatican II taught us Christians to realize more fully that we are called by our baptisms to change the systems that make people poor. Very few of us have made this teaching of Vatican II our own. We are so busy with our own lives on a day-to-day basis that the poor get ignored. In a word, they are crucified with Jesus on the cross of our indifference.

A momentary, sacred pause…

LEADER Jesus, your people call out for justice from the depths of despair. They call to you. Will you answer them? We know that your answer is us: we are sent to stop the crucifixion of the world. Give us the amazing grace and courage that we need to respond. Amen.

The Twelfth Station

Announcement of the Station

LEADER   The Twelfth Station: Jesus dies on the cross

Dialogue

LEADER   We adore you, O Christ, and we bless you.

ALL   Because by your holy cross, you have redeemed the world.

LEADER   Jesus, we believe in you and we love you. We have been moved by your powerful presence among us, and we have entered into your death ourselves, seeking to find in you the source of our life and love. May we freely give of our own lives for one another. May we be filled with the power of your grace.

Response (PSALM 130)

ALL   Help, GOD—the bottom has fallen out of my life!
Master, hear my cry for help!
Listen hard! Open your ears!
Listen to my cries for mercy.
If you, GOD, kept records on wrongdoings,
who would stand a chance?
As it turns out, forgiveness is your habit,
and that's why you're worshiped.
I pray to GOD—my life a prayer—
and wait for what he'll say and do.

My life's on the line before God, my Lord,
   waiting and watching till morning,
   waiting and watching till morning.
O Israel, wait and watch for GOD—
   with GOD's arrival comes love,
   with GOD's arrival comes generous redemption.
No doubt about it—he'll redeem Israel,
   buy back Israel from captivity to sin.

Reflection

LEADER   As Pope John was preparing to die, he told his closest
friends not to worry about him, because, he said, his bags
were packed! Like Jesus, Pope John trusted that God would
not abandon him. Let us pause on our way of the cross to
allow the reality of Jesus to enter deeply into our own souls.

ALL   (KNEEL FOR A MOMENT)

A momentary, sacred pause...

LEADER   Jesus, help us turn our hearts to you in prayer now as we
remember your death and prepare for your resurrection.
Increase our faith and help us see how our own dying to
self will lead to the same life-after-death that you promised.
Amen.

The Thirteenth Station

Announcement of the Station

LEADER   The Thirteenth Station: Jesus is taken down from the cross

Dialogue

LEADER   We adore you, O Christ, and we bless you.

ALL   Because by your holy cross, you have redeemed the world.

LEADER   Jesus, we are given to one another for love and care—just as you loved and cared for others, even while dying yourself. As your closest friends removed you from the cross and placed you in the grave, your mother and friend, Mary and John, were giving us an example: may we become each other's mothers, fathers, sons, and daughters ourselves. May we become the family of God! May we keep one another safe from harm and hold one another fast in the storms of life. And may we trust that your divine Spirit gives us the power to do this.

Response (PSALM 121)

ALL   I look up to the mountains;
     does my strength come from mountains?
No, my strength comes from GOD,
     who made heaven, and earth, and mountains.
He won't let you stumble,
     your Guardian God won't fall asleep.
Not on your life! Israel's
     Guardian will never doze or sleep.

GOD's your Guardian,
    right at your side to protect you—
Shielding you from sunstroke,
    sheltering you from moonstroke.
GOD guards you from every evil,
    he guards your very life.
He guards you when you leave and when you return,
    he guards you now, he guards you always.

Reflection

LEADER While it is true that Pope John XXIII and Vatican II called us
all to care for the men and women of the world who suffer
and are in pain, we know it is impossible for most of us to
leave our homes and do that in person. But there is another
call that is closer to home, a call to take care of each other
right here in the parish to which we belong. The Eucharist
we share makes us the body of Christ. It unites us. Just as
the grave of Jesus was not the final chapter in this story, so
disunity and human suffering are not the final chapter in our
story. God indeed is our keeper, but we are God's hands and
feet!

A momentary, sacred pause…

LEADER Jesus, we believe in you and we love you. We embrace your
presence in our hearts and lives. We accept with gratitude
your power to heal and forgive us. We embrace your presence in our Church. Renew it constantly in the vision and
energy of your Spirit. Amen.

The Fourteenth Station

Announcement of the Station

LEADER   The Fourteenth Station: Jesus is laid in the tomb

Dialogue

LEADER   We adore you, O Christ, and we bless you.

ALL   Because by your holy cross, you have redeemed the world.

LEADER   Jesus, our few moments here remembering your final days and nights is near an end, as you are being placed in the tomb by friends who loved you and believed in you. This journey for us has taken us back to your betrayals, trials, and violent death. We don't pretend to understand all these mysteries, but we do now see the connection between your journey and our own. May we remain conscious of your presence among us now so that we are always aware of our own power to teach, heal, and minister in your name. Amen.

Response (PSALM 23)

ALL   GOD, my shepherd!
    I don't need a thing.
You have bedded me down in lush meadows,
    you find me quiet pools to drink from.
True to your word, you let me catch my breath
    and send me in the right direction.
Even when the way goes through Death Valley,
I'm not afraid when you walk at my side.

Your trusty shepherd's crook makes me feel secure.
You serve me a six-course dinner
    right in front of my enemies.
You revive my drooping head;
    my cup brims with blessing.
Your beauty and love chase after me every day of my life.
I'm back home in the house of GOD for the rest of my life.

Reflection

LEADER In calling Vatican II, Pope John knew the Spirit would be with the Church and that the risen Christ would empower the Church to reform itself so dramatically that the world could be saved. Pope John dreamed of releasing to the world the saving and life-giving salvation of Jesus Christ. He hoped to make the world a more holy place, less filled with division and mistrust, and more filled with well-formed hearts and souls, eager to know God and to spread the word! Vatican II refocused us. Our real mission is to release into the world the powerful Spirit of Jesus! Let us now go about our work in the Church and the world aware of the connection and, indeed, determined to "spread the word!"

A momentary, sacred pause…

LEADER Even as we follow you to the tomb, Jesus, we know that you overcame death. By embracing the call to holiness given you by your Father, you saved us by your wonderful self-giving love. May we likewise learn to love selflessly. Amen.

A final moment
with Saint John XXIII

There was never anyone like Pope John in the entire history of the Church. Standing in the very place occupied by so many of his predecessors, he could see beyond them all. In speaking of his reasons for calling Vatican II, he once said, "We must shake off the imperial dust that has accumulated on the throne of St. Peter since Constantine" in the fourth century. In the spirit of Good Pope John, we too must stop looking among the dead for that which is living in the Church. We must embrace the work of the Spirit as it unfolds around us. We must seek life for the Church by looking forward, not backward.

Gather us together for the work of your kingdom,
O God, Grant us power, strength, love,
and patience. Lead us to do what is loving and good,
and to avoid what is hateful and evil. And give us
the happiness of being your disciples. Amen.